THE BOOK ON DISCRIMINATION

Real Life Stories of Struggles and Triumphs

Gaby Abdelgadir

10-10-10 Publishing

THE BOOK ON DISCRIMINATION – Real Life Stories Struggles and Triumphs

www.TheBookonDiscrimination.com

Copyright © 2020 by Gaby Abdelgadir

ISBN: 978-1-77277-384-2

Publisher
10-10-10 Publishing
Markham, ON
Canada

Printed in Canada and the United States of America

First 10-10-10 Publishing paperback edition October 2020

TABLE OF CONTENTS

Foreword   vii
Acknowledgements   ix

Chapter 1: What is Considered Discrimination?   **1**
Forward or Backward?   3
Definition of Discrimination   6
Who Suffers from Discrimination?   6

Chapter 2: Race Discrimination   **13**
Young Kids and Discrimination   15
What Happens When You Just Don't Know?   17
Discrimination in the Classroom: Black-on-Black   18
Lack of Awareness in Some Schools   22
Growing up in a Racist Family   26

Chapter 3: Workplace Discrimination   **37**
If You Are Not Part of the Solution, *You Are* Part of the
Problem!   39
Is Ignorance Really Bliss?   41
The Struggle of an Educated Woman   44
OMG! She is Black?!!   45
Racism Inside the Police Department? *What!*   46
Not Good Enough for Inclusion   48
Discrimination Inside Higher Education   49

Chapter 4: Cultural Discrimination   **57**
You Are Not Married Yet?   59
Being Single and Facing the Reality   60

Chapter 5: Mixed Race Families   **67**
When You Are Born of Mixed Race   69
Colored? What does It Even Mean?   70
I Never Thought About Giving My Adopted Daughter "The Talk"   73
Why Do I Look Different?   77
My Life Experiences of Racism: A Recollected Synopsis   79

Chapter 6: Status, Disability, and Appearance   **87**
Made Fun of for Not Having the Status   89
Disability and How Some People Are Treated   93

Chapter 7: Time to Bring Awareness, Equality, Acceptance, and Respect   **101**
Learn to ACCEPT, LOVE, and RESPECT Individuals for Who They Are   103

About the Author   109

I dedicate this book to every kid and every adult
who has been discriminated against, bullied,
or mistreated in any way.

FOREWORD

The Book on Discrimination: Real Life Stories of Struggles and Triumphs by Gaby Abdelgadir is intended to help you understand that, if you have been discriminated against, mistreated or bullied because of your skin color, race, culture, religion or status, you are not alone!

As you read the stories in this book, about all the struggles shared by kids and adults equally, you will understand the kinds of discrimination which cause separation, division, aggression, violence, abuse, rejection, arrogance, hatred, depression and even suicide.

You are programmed by your nation, culture, parents, and environment to discriminate against certain things and people, often unconsciously, and this results in your specific behavior towards others.

Gaby is constantly and tirelessly making a difference in the world. This book is proof of her commitment, dedication, and passion. She is an advocate for equality, fairness and kindness in the world by bringing awareness regarding prejudice, and its impact on society. By reading this book, you will learn the importance of loving every human being, regardless of race, culture, religion, status or skin color.

I consider *The Book on Discrimination* a must read!

Raymond Aaron
New York Times Bestselling Author

ACKNOWLEDGEMENTS

I would first like to take a moment to thank my publisher, Raymond Aaron, and his amazing team, for all their guidance and support. What I have learned from him about writing and marketing a book is invaluable.

I would like to acknowledge and thank my best friend, Thea Cosma, who pushed me to finish this book although I had it on hold due to Covid-19, and for her continuous support and encouragement.

I am always grateful to my good friend, Sahar Whelan, for her continuous support, friendship, and encouragement on my book project.

My sincere appreciation to my brother-in-law, Dawit Fessaha, for his continuous support and encouragement as a family member.

Many thanks to my mentor Gordon So for continuously pushing me to get out of my comfort zone.

My gratitude to my good friend, Angie Bianco (a.k.a. Italiana), for her continuous support and encouragement in writing this book.

I am grateful to my good friend, Tammy Williams, for keeping me accountable and for her continuous support.

My sincere gratitude to my good friend, Mebrat Males, for her continuous friendship, support, and encouragement.

I would like to give my gratitude to all the amazing individuals who have shared their stories in my book.

My utmost appreciation goes to:
Lester Bailey
Sahar Whelan
Tammy Williams
Dr. Anthony Hutchinson
Shaundi Goins
Michael Huggins
Cheryl Karina Bromfield
Sutha Shanmugarajah
Marcelle Wynter

I am very grateful to all the students from Grade 6 and above that I interviewed, who shared with me their discrimination and bullying struggles. (Names will not be included, to protect their identities.)

My gratitude goes to all the people I randomly interviewed in the mall, in the stores, on the train, and more.

CHAPTER ONE

WHAT IS CONSIDERED DISCRIMINATION?

"I walk slowly, but I never walk backward."
Abraham Lincoln

Forward or Backward?

I had started writing this book back in September 2019, and my goal was to publish it by the end of April 2020 or so, throwing a large launch party and all! My friends were so excited that they were making plans as to who would bring what food and drinks etc. for the launch!

Obviously, Covid-19 happened, and so I decided to postpone it until the issue of this virus is gone, and life becomes normal. Little did I know that this "normal" is not happening anytime soon!

But this chapter is NOT about Covid-19!

This chapter is about the craziness that has transpired since then. It is about what has happened in recent months, and keeps on happening, in the world! As a matter of fact, it is getting worse!

Racism! Unnecessary killing! Protests! Riots! Fights! Need I say more?

When are we going to move forward instead of going backward?

When are we going to look beyond someone's skin color, race, or culture?

Is this really happening in the 21st century? I mean, *really*?

When are we ALL really going to GROW UP?!

Ever since the brutal death of George Floyd, by police in Minneapolis, Minnesota, back in May 2020, I have seen horrible—I mean horrible—videos of similar cases.

I had stopped watching the news since 2012, so I haven't really been in the loop when it comes to murders and all the horrible things that have been happening; this was my first, in a very long time. If there was something important that family or friends believed I needed to know, they would call me. And that is only if something happens to someone I know, etc.

For the past few months, however, I have been bombarded by social media with news, videos, comments... I have watched videos that were so horrible that they made me sick to the extent that I threw up many, many times! I had no option but to private message people to stop sending me those type of videos. I eventually started blocking people who posted those types of videos and messages!

We have come to learn that "what we focus on, we attract." By no means am I saying that we should keep quiet or ignore—NO. But by spreading horrible videos and horrifying stories that happened years and years ago, in addition to the present, we are just attracting more of that. We should stop this craziness without multiplying the picture.

As if this is not enough... the fights and arguments on social media between people! Like me, there are a lot (both black and white) who strongly believe that "Black Lives Matter," while there are many, many who argue, and to them, "All Lives Matter."

I agree one hundred percent that "All Lives Matter," but what we are seeing now (and which has been happening frequently over the years, although not to the world's knowledge) is that the lives of "only" blacks and/or people of color are being wasted, the reason why "BLM."

The truth is that not only blacks have been attacked through the years. The Moslems have gone through it at one point or another, and so have the Jewish! There could be more that I am not aware of.

In my lifetime, I have worked in a few countries and alongside more than 300 nationalities, with different race, culture, religion, and status. I never saw any of them for their background, skin color, or their personal beliefs. I have always respected all of them, if they were good, respectful people.

So why can't everyone be like that? Why are we going backward?

I pray to God the Almighty, for LOVE, COMPASSION, KINDNESS, and RESPECT to fill up this planet.

Definition of Discrimination

The Oxford dictionary describes the word "discrimination" as follows:

"Treating a person or a particular group of people differently, especially in a worse way from the way in which you treat other people, because of their skin color, sex, sexuality, racial background, age and more."

In my personal opinion, discrimination is a lot more, and deeper than just how all the dictionaries describe it. It is not only about treating people differently. There is hate, bullying, and criminal activity involved in a lot of cases.

In all cases, discrimination causes pain, suffering, depression, anxiety and in worse cases, suicide!!

That is why I am passionately writing this book to bring awareness and education regarding this particular issue in our society, especially after seeing so many youngsters ending their lives!!

****

Who Suffers from Discrimination?

- People with different skin color.
- People with different race.
- People of mixed race.
- People with different religious beliefs.
- People with disabilities.

- People with a different accent.
- People who are immigrants.
- People who are poor.
- People who are not so good looking.
- People who are not educated.

The list could go on...

Here are a few examples of what discrimination looks like:

One of my personal examples of discrimination is when I go to a restaurant with my boss or my colleagues, who happen to be mostly Caucasians. The waitress would come in and would have such a big smile on her face when taking orders from them, and it seemed that the smile would fade as soon as it was my turn to order! It used to make me angry! I mean, really angry! And sad!

I remember, years ago, one waitress who actually was black, and when she was taking my order, not only did she have a straight face, but she was angry! Her face completely changed when she went around the table; she had a huge smile taking the other team members' orders! I was so mad, and I made up my mind to teach her a lesson after work.

I went to the restaurant after work and asked for the manager, and I had him call the particular waitress in. I told her how bad she treated me and that she needs to change her attitude and be good to everyone! Not only for the white skin! I said to her, "How would you feel if someone treated you the same, and gave you a dirty look at a restaurant just because you are black?" She tried to deny it, but I cut her off immediately.

Now, I don't get upset at all. On the contrary, I smile at them (even if they treat me differently), I compliment them, and the mood completely changes!

I am positive that my new approach is helping a lot of them change their attitude!

Another kind of discrimination is when someone is walking with their disabled child, and people stare at them in a weird way, with no compassion! I know firsthand because I know a lot of people who have a severely disabled child, and nobody wants to get close to them, especially when they are out at parks or whenever they are in the mall. It is so sad and *pathetic*!

It is discrimination when a parent treats her kids' friends differently based on their race!

And then there is discrimination at the workplace, employees being discriminated against because of either their race, culture, or religion! Or discrimination between male and female!

Should I go on?   Nope, I think it is enough for now.

Keep reading, and you will understand what I am talking about.

Notes

_____

_____

_____

_____

_____

_____

_____

_____

_____

_____

_____

_____

_____

_____

_____

_____

_____

_____

_____

_____

_____

_____

Notes

_____

_____

_____

_____

_____

_____

_____

_____

_____

_____

_____

_____

_____

_____

_____

_____

_____

_____

_____

_____

_____

Notes

Notes

_____

_____

_____

_____

_____

_____

_____

_____

_____

_____

_____

_____

_____

_____

_____

_____

_____

_____

_____

_____

CHAPTER TWO

RACE DISCRIMINATION

*"I hate race discrimination most intensely and in all its
Manifestations. I have fought it all during my life; I fight now,
and will do so until the end of my days."*
Nelson Mandela

Young Kids and Discrimination

Some Will Say They Know Our Pain; Some Believe It Doesn't Exist
By Tammy Williams

Over 40 years ago, in a small Northern Ontario city called Sudbury, during the spring rainy season, the unthinkable happened. It was the kind of day where you have to be the sunshine, a day full of hope and promise. For a classroom of Grade-1 students, recess was so much fun as we played in the puddles and giggled.

The bell rang, ending the morning recess. We ran inside and took off our wet clothes and footwear. Once in the classroom, we were instructed to sit at the round tables, with our heads resting on our arms on the table.

What happened next would forever change me. The teacher asked everyone who wore rubber boots to please come to the floor and make a circle for reading time. That day, I didn't wear my rubber boots. I was left at the table all by myself while the rest of the class took part in reading time. *Coincidence*? I think not. I was incredibly sad.

The next bell rang, and it was lunch time. The afternoon went by really slow for me. The dismissal bell couldn't have come soon enough.

When I reached home, my mom knew something was wrong; I cried uncontrollably.

Finally, after I stopped crying, I told my mom what had happened. My mom went to school with me the next day and made sure that the teacher had to apologize to me.

As a little girl, I didn't know what I experienced. As I got older, I realized it was a *racist* act. A little innocent 6-year-old, who happened to be **the only black** in the class, who also was not wearing rain boots.

I was too young to understand, but I knew I was different and that I was going to have to be strong.

Tammy Williams
Dream Builder
IG tammyunlimited
Founder of Women Champagne and Real Estate
IG Account champagnelivingbytammy
FB Women Champagne and Real Estate
tammywomenchampagne@gmail.com

What Happens When You Just Don't Know?
By Lester Bailey

Let me tell you a story about myself.

I was recently asked a question by a great friend of mine: "Have you ever been confronted with racism and/or prejudice?" I then looked around my house—at the ceiling, at the floor—and it amazed me how many stories I had of living through racism and prejudice.

My story begins in the early 1960s, living in Chicago in the South Shore area. My mother moved us into the South Shore area, and we were the first black family living in the neighborhood. I didn't know what that meant until my first day of being confronted with racism and prejudice.

I was in 2nd grade at grammar school when I met this young girl. She was the prettiest girl to me at the time. It was the 1st day of class, and after the teacher introduced me to the class, she told me to take a seat. So, I went to sit next to the pretty girl. Now, me being the only black child in the classroom, I thought it was okay to sit next to her. The other children in the classroom, however, didn't want me to sit next to anybody. They told me they don't sit next to *niggers*! I didn't understand what they meant, and I told them I was no nigger. They said, "Yes, you are you are black!"

Until then, nobody had ever told me that I was black. Everyone looked the same to me, and I had no knowledge about being black. That day awakened me to "color." When I finally got to meet that little girl, and we liked each other, the boys in the classroom began to beat me up and chase me home regularly!

Lester Bailey – Retired Police Officer
Entrepreneur/International Best-Selling Author

****

Discrimination in the Classroom: Black-on-Black
By Cheryl Karina Bromfield

"I've learned that people will forget what you said, people will forget what you did, but people will never forget how you made them feel."

Those are the words of one of my mentors, the awe-inspiring Maya Angelou; and wow, do those words ever ring true, time and time again, and undoubtedly take me back 30 plus years ago, sitting in my Grade-2 classroom. I can remember instinctively how I felt in that space, a space that should feel full of life, motivation, creativity, and joy. For me, it breathed an emptiness, darkness, and an eternity that in my little body, didn't seem like it would go away any time soon.

This cold energy was made possible through the presence of my least favorite teacher. This teacher, whether she realized it or not, gave me a taste in my mouth, in the crevices of my spirit, which I will never forget. It was a dismal chapter in my development. I can honestly and painfully say that it stands out as my personal encounter with the ugly face of discrimination.

Mrs. F. seemed to target me with annoyed glances and harsh criticism more than any of my peers. In her presence, I felt inferior, dirty, worthless, inadequate, incapable, and even gross. I felt ashamed for the color of my skin in her presence, when I should have felt proud. Day in and day out, I never felt I could perform anything correctly to her seemingly unattainable standards.

You would think, as a black child at the start of the school year, I would feel a surge of excitement, sense of connection, motherly affection, and/or compassion from this—a *Black teacher*. Initially, I did at the sight of her, but what I thought I would receive was not what I expected, and quickly I might add once she opened her mouth or her eyes met mine.

Mrs. F.'s countenance alone said, *"Don't mess with me, don't cross me, and if you cross me, I'll make you feel the guilt every single day."* When she lost her temper, how could one forget her slapping her desk or that of a student's, with a long, wooden ruler. When that ruler hit whatever, my heart skipped a beat, and all of us innocent children's hearts must have, in unison, and audible to all of our ears telepathically. Anxiety surged through my being every time. It was as though I blamed myself for her reactions even if they had nothing to do with me directly. This unexpected reaction from Mrs. F. created a climate of fear in the room, which was ever so thick in the air. I dreaded entering this room each day, but as was my nature and because I didn't know better, I put up with it, feeling there was no way out.

I remember something as simple as all of us completing a spelling test. On this particular occasion, I lingered to finish mine. I was one of the ones who, because I was such a perfectionist, hung on to my test until I felt I had answered everything to the best of my ability. It seemed Mrs. F. didn't like this, as she happily retrieved the tests of those around me, and when she came toward me, she let out a sigh and asked, "Cheryl, are you finished yet?" with a slightly annoyed stare. Because of her attitude, I felt a degree of fear and intimidation, and I hurried to hand over my test. She would grab it with a serious face and a thanks uttered under her breath, which you could barely hear. I'll never forget when she would conduct math lessons and select students to go up to the board to write answers. She seemed to enjoy letting the students she favored give their answers and praise them with a brief smile. To see her smile was a miracle! It was such a rarity. She would select me but not with the same warmth. There was the serious face again, almost anticipating my failure, and I reacted physiologically with a rapid heartbeat and sweaty armpits. I did my best. Sometimes I got it wrong, and on this one occasion, she had me stay up there until I got it right. She hovered behind me in a stern manner, impatiently. How intimidating! I remember the helpless stares of my peers, looking like they wished they could rescue me from the spotlight. I honestly felt like she enjoyed humiliating the black child, one of the few. I thought I would melt. Back at my desk, I exhaled.

The way Mrs. F. looked at me, or sometimes interacted with me, appeared as though she was experiencing a bad, sour taste, an undesirable flavor hitting her taste buds. There was an undeniable, impeccable, impenetrable feeling of shame every time she gave that blue-eyed, blonde-haired boy or girl praise and a smile. When turning to me, it was coldness—an obvious contrast. My conclusion, as young as I was, was that I was being betrayed by my own, compared with others, and discriminated against. Why me? I would often ask myself and my mother tearfully. If Mrs. F. felt she had to push her *own* through tough love—if that was her philosophy of teaching—it failed; it failed miserably. After that year, I didn't have a healthy sense of myself, since I felt utterly disempowered.

I was a good girl, focused, kind to my peers, and always willing to learn and improve. She had no reason to treat me the way she did. I silently suffered and just strived to get through each day and do my best to please her. I did not have the skills back then to deal with her discrimination, but I do, today, especially as an educator myself. I see through different lenses by not showing favoritism whatsoever, but rather love, acceptance, and treating all equally. Do I feel a special connection to my Afro-Caribbean Canadian students? Of course! I make certain not to make them feel inferior, but rather as successful, as full of potential, and as worthy of praise as their fellow peers. My rescuer, the following year, in grade 3, was a black teacher who exercised all of the above with a motherly touch. She inspires my approach today. My teaching philosophy is about inclusion, and because I am a lover of God, He shines through, and my goal is that all my students feel that warmth. After all, in my eyes, I am a third parent, whose job is to educate, and most importantly, to love.

Cheryl Karina Bromfield
Author, Teacher, Founder of Amaziah

Lack of Awareness in Some Schools

There was this animosity between two teachers in the Catholic school that my son went to. Both were Caucasians. One taught Grade 2, and the other was teaching Grade 3. In Grade 2, his teacher really liked him, as he was a good listener and got straight A's every time. She never looked at him as a black kid, and treated him equally. His final Grade 2 results were all A+ in every single subject. I was so proud of him!

Then, the following year, when he started Grade 3, the other teacher, who hated the Grade 2 teacher, made his year very miserable, as she treated him so bad and discriminated against him every single day. Even though he did great in his tests and exams, she always had to find a way for him to not get a single "A." One day, he came home crying and told me everything this teacher had been doing to him.

I was really shocked and upset. I told him that I would take care of it. The next day, I went to the principal's office and had the principal call that teacher. Needless to say, she was horrified to see an angry woman, and she quietly declined that she was treating my son badly. I wouldn't take that, and I told her that if she EVER mistreated him or give him wrong grades or even looked at him in any bad way, not only would I sue her, but I would share the story at every television and radio station in the country.

The teacher started being nicer to him since then!

This issue may actually have been payback of some sort to the Grade 2 teacher, but how stupid is it to make an innocent kid pay for your personal issues?

****

I interviewed many, many students between grades 6 and 12, as well as some graduates, and here are a few of their responses:

****

I was one of 2 black kids in the classroom in Grade 8, and 2 of our teachers always picked on us. They used to embarrass us in front of the whole class if any our test results were not above 60% average. It would have been okay if they did it for everyone else, but they didn't. There was this white kid who barely got 50%, but he was never told off in front of everyone! It hurt and made us feel like we were not equal to others!

****

My parents are originally from Somalia, but I was born here, and I am first generation Canadian. I went to public schools, and from Grade 1 until Grade 8, I was bullied and called names all the time. A few of the kids sometimes used to corner and punch me! I started to hate school, and it affected my self-confidence.

I told the teachers and the principal, but they always ignored my complaints. Then, the summer before high school, my dad registered me for karate classes to learn to defend myself, and that was the best thing that ever happened to me! When we started high school, the same boys cornered me on the first day of Grade 9! They were to learn the lesson of their lives as I tackled each one and left them with bruises! The next morning, all of a sudden, they wanted to be friends with me!

* *

We are from the Philippines, and I was 9 years old when we came to Canada. My parents immediately registered me at a Catholic school. At the time, I didn't have the same accent as the other kids, and I was always made fun of by the kids. I used to go home and cry. My parents went and complained to the principal. Nothing changed. One of my teachers used to make me repeat a sentence many times, embarrassing me, and the whole class used to laugh at me. I hated that teacher! By the time I was in high school, my accent had improved a lot and things got better. But I still was getting jokes about my country and culture!

* *

As you can see, I am Chinese. The first weird question I got asked by one teacher, when I was in senior school, was, "Are you from the rich part or the poor part of China?" I was shocked and asked her what she meant. She said, "I heard that apart from Hong Kong, the rest of China is very poor!" How stupid was that? I then asked her if she had ever traveled to China, and she said that she had never been out of Canada or the USA! And what the hell was this ignorant woman talking about? I was furious and told my dad when I got home! To my surprise, my dad burst into laughter. When I asked him what was so funny about that, he said, "Son, you can't be upset with ignorant people; you either feel sorry for them, or if they are open, you educate them." That was one of the greatest lessons I learned that helped me in my future.

****

We are from Pakistan, and we immigrated to Canada when my siblings and I were little. We are Moslems, and when I turned 10, I started wearing long skirts, dresses, and long sleeve shirts. I also wore scarfs covering my hair. I was always looked down on, by even the principal. He never looked me in the eye and never listened to my complaints. My English teacher was so nice, and she always complimented me, which was helpful and good for my self-confidence. I was not the only kid that dressed the way I did, but they were not in the same class, and they were older. I was called names by some kids and never got invited to birthday parties, etc. Some kids even used to make funny jokes about my religion and Prophet Mohammed! That was really, really upsetting, and it put me into isolation for a while. I really felt sad and lonely most of the time during my junior school years. High school was a little better, and I made some friends who were actually Christians! It felt good that they didn't discriminate against me. The teachers were nice, and life started to get better.

* *

These were a very few selected from the many youngsters I interviewed.

My question is: Shouldn't there be leadership training dedicated to schools, their principals, and teachers - to help them teach all the kids to stop discrimination and bullying? As a matter of fact, shouldn't the government make that a LAW?

Having shared all the above stories, I have to give credit to all the amazing teachers out there (I know quite a few!) that treat their students like their own children and not only provide education, but give their students a lots of love.

* *

Growing up in a Racist Family

Before I even share other people's stories, let me tell you about my own parents!

My father was of Turkish origin, whose family immigrated to Sudan when he was young. In Sudan, he met my mother, who was Ethiopian.

Back in the 80s, there was some chaos in the country, and every single person needed a new identity card. I was working for UNICEF then, and I remember that they sent us with a driver, in groups, to get new photos and identity cards.

One Friday afternoon, my father came to visit us as usual but was angry and shaking! We were shocked, as he usually was a very happy man. My mom asked what was wrong, and here is what he said "I had the driver drop me off to buy fruits, and while walking, a tiny black soldier, holding a machine gun, stopped me and asked for my identity!!!" My mom then replied, "So, what is the problem? Everyone is supposed to show their identity card everywhere when asked." Then came the shock: "No black person asks me for my identity!" "So, what did you say to him?" I asked. His reply was, "I told him that he should get out of my way and move on, and that we owned 30 slaves like him! And that we only gave them freedom 20 years ago!" He was still angry and shaking!

This, coming from a man who married an African woman!!!!! And then there is the story of my mom.

She had moved to Ethiopia in the 90s and, at the time, I was working in UAE, so I visited her every year, and she visited other times.

On one of my visits, one of her cousins brought her husband to introduce him to her. The man was very successful, a real gentleman and very polite. He walked with a Black Label Whisky (a tradition when you visit people you respect).

The man was really a very dark-skinned Ethiopian. After the introductions, everyone sat down. Drinks were offered. I could see my mom's cousin (the wife), and that she was scared. I would quickly know why.

My mom then slowly but firmly asked him, "Are you clean?" He answered, "What do you mean, Madam?" The wife answered, "Yes, he is." My mom said, "I didn't ask you!" She turned to the man and asked him to list his background, seven generations back. The man's face changed, and anger was building, but then he quickly sighed and smiled. (Later, I learned that he had been warned of what a tough woman and how hard to please my mom was, and to be patient with her and answer all her questions.) He did, and my mom seemed pleased with his answer, and the celebration of food, etc. started.

But I couldn't get over that conversation, and it was in my mind, bothering me for the longest period!

I am so forever grateful that I didn't inherit any of that, and that I turned out to be a very different and open-minded woman compared to both my parents.

I turned out to be very loving and caring to all kinds of people, regardless of their background, race, religion, or culture, as long as we shared the same principles in life and were on the same frequency!

****

One story that I will always remember is about a colleague I had while working for Union Carbide Sudan in Khartoum.

She was Sudanese, with white skin color and very beautiful long black hair. She ended up falling in love with a very successful and wealthy businessman, and he wanted to marry her. The problem for her family was that he was really dark skinned and had course hair.

I remember one morning when she called me to an empty boardroom, closed the door, and started bawling her eyes out! I was so sad to see her like that, and when I asked her what had happened, her response in between sobs was, "My parents don't want me to marry him because he is too dark skinned. My mom said to me, 'You can't expect me to be walking around with little black kids with course hair.'"

Do I call this ignorance, stupidity, reckless, or what? I sat down, trying to absorb what I had just heard, and after a bit of silence, I asked her what she was planning to do. She said that she was going to marry him no matter what—even if she got kicked out of the house!

Well, she ended up marrying him (the parents attended although not very pleased) and had 2 beautiful children and a happy life!

****

What about some families who are not only racists but try to influence their kids to follow suit?

Here are some stories:

In high school, one male kid really wanted to hang around some popular kids who were a mix of races. He couldn't. When I asked him why not, he told me that if his father found out that he was hanging around with Asians and Black kids, he would take luxuries away from him - a car his father had bought him, and all the designer clothes, etc. So, he only hung around with the white kids! "There were so many cool kids that I really wanted to be friends with but couldn't. Now that I am an adult, independent, and living my life, I have a few Black and Asian friends! It is freeing!"

****

A Moslem girl really liked this boy in high school when they were in Grade 10, and started hanging around him and his friends. This boy was "white and Christian." Someone told her father that his daughter was being a bad example to their community, because she was hanging around these white Christian and Jewish boys. Not only did she get the beating of her life when she got home, she was banned from going to school, and the father hired a teacher and had her homeschooled!

"I left home when I turned 19. I stayed with friends until I got a job, and eventually was able to move into my own place. Guess what? I am friends with all kinds of great kids my age, Moslems,

Christians, Jews, Hindus, Buddhists, and believe it or not, an atheist!" she giggled. "I enjoy our conversations about our personal religious beliefs, cultures, and so on. Yes, sometimes we argue, but we end up agreeing to disagree, and respecting one another. In my personal opinion, to hell with rules and regulations!" she said.

"My father doesn't talk to me now, and I am not allowed to visit my mom and siblings. Some of them secretly meet me and keep in touch. I miss being a part of my family, and while I love and respect my religion, I refuse to be dictated as to who I should and should not befriend!"

****

In one of the prestigious high schools, there were 7 friends. They were 2 Koreans, 2 Blacks, 1 Latin, and 2 Caucasians. They became inseparable! They always celebrated their birthdays by having a big party and spending the night at the birthday kid's home. All were good, with the exception of one of the Caucasian kids. When the friends told him, "So, we are spending the night at your place?" The kid bent his head down and, all of a sudden, he was incredibly sad. The rest were surprised and asked him what had happened. His response was, "My mom will not allow Black kids to sleep over!" This was followed by silence. They still celebrated outside, but obviously, even the other kids who were allowed, refused to go to his house for a sleepover, in support of their Black friends.

How did the 2 Black kids feel? No comment!!! The good news here is that the kid didn't believe in discrimination, and never changed toward his Black friends.

****

I am a first generation Canadian as I was born here. My parents are from Eritrea. In school, there were more than a handful Eritreans, Ethiopians, and Somalis. My grandmother, however, never wanted me to befriend the Ethiopians and Somalis. When I asked her why, she really had no answer that was convincing to me. Luckily, my father was on my side and told me that as long as they were all good kids and came from decent families, I could befriend anyone I wanted. That didn't make my grandma happy.

Keep reading more stories...

Notes

_____

_____

_____

_____

_____

_____

_____

_____

_____

_____

_____

_____

_____

_____

_____

_____

_____

_____

_____

_____

_____

_____

_____

_____

Notes

Notes

Notes

CHAPTER THREE

WORKPLACE DISCRIMINATION

*"A change in skin color doesn't
change the individual.
Get to know them for their identity and talent
not for their looks, race or culture."*
Gaby Abdelgadir

If You Are Not Part of the Solution, You Are Part of the Problem!
By Marcelle Wynter

I worked for a very prestigious university in the human resources department, and a big telecommunications company was called in to help and was working with the university's IT department. The telecom employee had been in the office the previous day, and I noticed that he was paying close attention to me without addressing me, but I did not think too much of it. The next day he came back with the university IT employee and remarked that he had brought his "Nigger" with him.

I heard a lot of gasps from my co-workers, and the IT employee was noticeably embarrassed. None of these adults spoke to this telecom worker to defend me. I did not speak because I knew that the telecom employee wanted me to be upset. The word, to me, describes the mentality of the man using it, so I was not too disturbed. The next day, I was called into both my manager's office and the director's office, and both people told me that the word that was obviously used against me *"was not meant to be a racial slur."* I did not report the incident, and I have never reported incidences of this sort in my 17 years of working in that environment, and that was not the first or the last racial slur that had been thrown at me. One of my co-workers, who never spoke up when the incidents occurred, always went to complain on my behalf. I was very offended when the director and the manager both told me that the comment was not a racial slur. I sent a letter to the telecom company, advising them that I was a very good employee and that they needed to have some diversity training for their staff, and that things needed to change. I did receive a response but, of course, everything was always watered down.

I was alone and nobody would help me. I eventually left my position due to the stress and the negativity that was impacting my health.

I want to note that discrimination is real, but of course there are a lot of different types of discrimination, and this is just one of them. Racism is big because it affects a race of people who do not have the power to fight an establishment that has been against them all along. I hope that if we get to know one another and realize that we have much more in common than we differ, we will understand that we should celebrate our differences rather than fearing them.

Marcelle Wynter
Author

Is Ignorance Really Bliss?

My experience on my job search in Canada

"What was your background again?"

I was asked by that one executive for the third time in 45 minutes!

I was on a temporary job and in search of a full-time opportunity. I saw a great position online and applied for it. Then I forgot about it.

Three weeks later, I received a call from their human resources department, and I was scheduled for an hour interview. On my scheduled day, I met with two wonderful ladies who were senior human resources members. They informed me that 380 people had applied for that position, and that I was narrowed down to the top 10! 380? I was surprised and proud that I had made it to the top 10. They told me they would get in touch with me.

As it turned out, I made it to the top four and was scheduled to be interviewed by a couple of senior people, and if I made it, then I would interview with 2 executives.

Needless to say, my second interview went very well, and I made it to the top 2 and was ready to be interviewed by the 2 executives.

I and a brunette with beautiful green eyes were the winners from 380 applicants.

It was time for my interview with the 2 executives, and to make it easier, I am going to call them JJ and KJ.

JJ was impatient, arrogant, and lacked general knowledge (Yes, even with his high position!). KJ, on the other hand, was calm, collected, and polite. Here is how some of the interview went:

JJ: Where are you from originally?

Me: Sudan.

JJ: Where is that???

KJ: It's in Africa. Remember MS who used to work with us? He was Sudanese.

JJ: That black man? *He was so black that you could only see his teeth in a blackout!*

KJ: His face, red from embarrassment, managed to say, "He was the best."

Me: Shocked and probably open-mouthed…

JJ: Not too impressed by my family name, he asked me how it was pronounced.

KJ: Ab del gadir… "Did I get it right?" he asked me with a smile.

Me: Absolutely. That's how it is pronounced.

JJ: Tried to pronounce it a few times without success and was frustrated.

KJ: It was a pleasure meeting you, Gaby, and we will be in touch once we decide.

JJ: Yes. What was your background again?

KJ: I will explain. We have a meeting waiting for us now.

In conclusion, the beautiful, white, brunette with the green eyes was offered the position. Later, I met KJ downtown while we were both walking opposite ways. He stopped and shook my hand and asked how I was doing. He also told me that they had made a huge mistake with their choice, and that the lady they chose over me was fired within her first 5 weeks!!

After that experience, I promised myself that no matter what situation I may be in, I would never work with someone like JJ!!!

I ended up getting hired full-time with a prestigious company, working with the best executives, team, and group that anyone could dream of.

Keep reading; there is a lot more.

The Struggle of an Educated Woman
By Sahar Whelan

Does having a PhD eliminate you from being discriminated against?

My beloved late mom, Dr. Tahia Elguindi, had her PhD in biochemistry at the age of 26. She immigrated to Canada in 1970. She found *a j*ob that required a person to research exactly what her PhD thesis was about. She thought for sure that she would be hired. When she was in the interview, the man told her, "You are perfect for the job, and you are the best candidate, but I can't hire you."

Tahia Elguindi, surprised, asked why.

The man told her, "Because you are from Egypt, and I am Jewish, so it is not right."

My mom was devastated at this reality. Moving forward, she applied for jobs and hid the fact that she had a hard-earned master's degree and PhD. So, to feed her family, she worked as a lab technician, where they treated her badly and upset her to the point that one day, she ran down the stairs to get away from their bullying, fell down the stairs, hurt her ankle, and then couldn't walk! So, they fired her.

That's what discrimination does!!!!

Sahar Whelan, RPh, BScPhm, MScPhm
Director, Concord Specialty Pharmacy

OMG! She is Black?!!

In most of my jobs, I was on the phone a lot: scheduling appointments, board meetings, event planning, travel arrangements, and more.

In one of my jobs, a lot of executives from top industries used to call me if my boss didn't pick up his phone. I always covered up for him. Well, I must admit that sometimes I had to lie, because he would be sitting there but didn't want to talk to a particular person at a particular time.

One of these executives was always asking me over the phone what my background was. And my reply always was, "You will have to guess," and I never told him anything about my origin or my background.

On every call, he would ask, "Why is it that you can't tell me where you are from? And I would say, "Guess." He made many guesses, to no avail. "It's your accent...Ukraine?" "No." "Bulgaria?" "No." I think he must have mentioned almost all of Eastern Europe, which was really surprising to me.

About a year or so later, he came to our office. He walked by me and went straight to my boss's office, and he asked out loud, "So, where is this Gaby?" My boss replied, "She is right behind you; you just passed by her."

The man turned around to look at me, and then said out loud (kind of with disappointment), "OMG! She is Black?? You should have seen the shock and silence that took place at our office! No comment. Most of the staff on the floor heard him. They all turned to look at me, worried and in shock. I smiled at all of them and slowly whispered, "It's okay; I am not upset. I love who I am and where I came from." There was a look of relief on their faces. My boss came to apologize to me after this guy left. He was so embarrassed.

My response to someone like that would be a quote by William Shakespeare: *"Ignorance is the curse of God; knowledge is the wing wherewith we fly to Heaven."*

****

Racism Inside the Police Department? *What!*
By Lester Bailey

In the late 80s, I joined the Chicago Police Department as a rookie, and I had been on the streets for about six months. Again, I was confronted with racism and prejudice by a fellow officer. The first time I met him, he did not want to work with me. I thought it was only because I was a rookie. Later, I found out that this had nothing to do with why he didn't want to work with me.

One day, another officer and I happened to be doing paperwork on the street when we observed two young people walking. Another squad car came to the scene and stopped the two kids (a young white female and a young black male), who were walking down the street at 61st and Green. He got out of the car and asked the young black boy why he was out there with a white girl. The boy replied that she was his girlfriend. Then he asked the white girl why she was out there with this nigger boy. That didn't make me feel good! She answered that he was her boyfriend. The officer went back to the black kid and slapped him, telling him that he was never to be with a white woman in his entire life. He then put handcuffs on him and ordered the girl to get into the back of the squad car. He told her that he would drive her home as she had no business to ever again be seen with somebody black and beneath her race! He told the black kid that he was going to put him in jail on a trumped-up charge.

That is when I jumped out the squad car and told him off. I told him that he should never treat him or any other black person like that ever again! Of course, we argued on the street for a little while, and the black kid was able to go home with his girlfriend. My partner (who was a white officer and observed the whole scenario) and I agreed that we would never let somebody treat someone like that.

Of course, the racist white officer and I never got along! Once, we almost got into a fight at the station, regarding his prejudice and racism, and how low he thought of black people. Eventually, he got transferred out to other districts. A triumph!

I could tell you hundreds of stories that I have experienced and witnessed.

Lester Bailey – Retired Officer
Entrepreneur/International Bestselling Author

Not Good Enough for Inclusion

I was once working at a prestigious corporate company, and I was the only black lady in the office.

We had a lot of sports fans in the office. I mean, serious fans! Including all executives!

During the game season, one of the executives always gave tickets to the team.

Except me!

I always kept working while all the *"Thank you! Wow! Much appreciated!"* etc. etc. was going on, and never raised my head to look around! One of the team once said to me, "Aw, Gaby, do you want to go watch the game? You can take mine, and I can even get you a second one to take Michael with you (my son)." I thought that was so sweet, but I couldn't do that. I thanked him and told him that he should go and have fun, as I had a lot of work at home.

One day, I decided to raise my head (just for the sake of curiosity) while the same executive was handing out tickets, just to find out that he was looking at me sideways while handing the tickets to all. I guess he wanted to see my reaction. I gave him a smile— a sarcastic one (if you can read expressions!).

I never really see any difference between me and others until this kind of thing happens.

As a black woman, am I not good enough to attend a game? Silence is golden!

****

Discrimination Inside Higher Education
By Shaundi Goins

I worked for an organization for nearly four years as a college recruiter and academic counselor. I was the best in the entire university in both my roles. I was not only respected by my students but held in high esteem among my peers, faculty, and staff. I was the best in my career in higher education because I loved serving students to help them live a successful and fulfilling lifestyle. No one was more passionate and determined or lived to serve their students as a servant and transformation leader, than me.

Midway through my career as a college recruiter and academic counselor, the office of admissions was divided into two departments: the admissions team, was charged with enrolling new students; and the academic counseling team, which worked with current students from day one until graduation. Despite my team (the admissions team had the best recruiters the university had ever employed), I was transferred to the academic counseling team. Why the university's president at the time decided to transfer me to the academic counseling team instead of enrolling new college students, is a mystery to me even today. But because I love what I do for my students, I accepted my new role and performed at the highest standard.

Before the changes were made by the president, the admissions and academic department was led by the executive director of admissions and academic counseling. Once the departments were split into two, the academic team was led by one of the university's vice presidents. During this time, I wanted to get promoted as a senior academic advisor. I figured, what the hell; since I was no longer in the admissions department, it was time for me to assume a leadership role as a senior academic advisor. At that time, the university had never had a "senior" counselor role with the admissions or academic counseling department, but as part of the new changes within the departments, the president decided to hire and/or promote senior admissions and academic counselors. When I found out about the news, I was excited. I was the most tenured, talented, skilled, and by far the most qualified employee within our department. When I let my manager know I was applying for the position, she made me feel like I was a good candidate for the role. I just knew the senior academic counselor position would be mine. A couple of weeks later, I was betrayed by the university that I gave my life to.

On a Monday morning, my manager made an announcement that sent shockwaves throughout the entire university. A new senior academic advisor was hired. However, no one in our department earned the promotion, not even me. The person they put into the role had a Ph.D. and was in charge of an entirely different department—a department that had nothing to do with academic counseling. When it was announced that this person would be our supervisor, it was also announced by our department head that the decision was final. This meant that no one was legally able to apply and interview for the position. My department head knew who she was going to place in that senior counseling position, and never had any intention of promoting me. Yes, she held me back. She held back the best admissions and academic counselor the university had ever employed. I never claimed to be the best at my position, but the former university's president, vice president, all the deans, faculty, and staff said, "Shaundi, you are the best person we have ever had in your role." My colleagues also said that I was the best! Despite my being the best fit for the role, it was given to someone that had no clue about advising college students. Because of her lack of experience in this department, and it being a new role, guess who had to train her to become my supervisor?

Everyone I worked with at the university was upset by this decision. Many of my colleagues felt that if the university did not see my value and leadership skills to lead the academic counseling team, then it may be time to work for a college or university that would celebrate my skills that create results for its students and the school.

I was taught by my mentor a long time ago: "If you have skills to help an organization thrive, you will never have to worry about money." A few months later, after working as an academic counselor, I received a promotion as an assistant director of admissions.

What my former employer did to me, and to other great employees of the university, was highly unethical. Instead of placing the right candidates for leadership roles, they played the "favoritism" card, and hired and promoted their friends or favorite employees. The great John C. Maxwell once said, *"Everything rises and falls on leadership."* The university I left is on the verge of closing because of poor leadership decisions.

Seven years ago, students wanted to be a part of the esteemed university. Today, prospective students no longer see the value of attending the university. Many current students are eager to graduate or transfer to another high education institution that will help them achieve their academic goals. It is a sad story, right?

Discrimination is real today, in the 21st century. I am here to tell you today: "Always go where you are celebrated, and not just tolerated. Do everything you can to become an expert in your life's work. If your current employer does not see your worth, trust me, another organization will. If you feel you don't have the marketing skills to promote yourself to other companies, do yourself a huge favor and invest in a successful high-performance consultant that has a proven track record in helping others achieve greatness in their professional lives."

Sending you love, light, and magic.

Shaundi Goins
Founder/CEO of SHAUNDI GOINS COACHING GROUP
Website: www.shaundigoins.com
Email: shaundigoins23@gmail.com

Notes

Notes

_____

_____

_____

_____

_____

_____

_____

_____

_____

_____

_____

_____

_____

_____

_____

_____

_____

_____

_____

Notes

Notes

CHAPTER FOUR

CULTURAL DISCRIMINATION

"I am very proud to be Black, but Black is not all I am.
That's my cultural historical background, my genetic makeup,
but it's not all of who I am,
nor is it the basis from which I answer every question."
Denzel Washington

You Are Not Married Yet?

This is what I heard over and over again!

The stupidest culture, I have to say, is where a girl has to be married in her early twenties at the latest! Why? In some cultures, it brings shame to the family when a girl is not married while very young!

I was attending the wedding of the daughter of one of my mom's friend's. I was 27 years old. The girl getting married was 23, and apparently even being 23 was kind of later for marriage.

One of the older ladies that my mom knew very well, asked me out loud, "How old are you now?" I replied that I was 27. She had a look of disgust on her face, and she asked me, "How come you are not married yet? Do none of your co-workers want to marry you?"

I was so shocked!! I got really mad but kept quiet. She wouldn't let it go, and asked, "No man has ever asked you to marry him?" Then I couldn't keep quiet; I snapped at her, "What if I don't want to marry? I have a great job, I make good money, and I travel every year, so why do I need a marriage?" That was a shocker that would go around in gossip for a very long time! But I had to shut her up.

This woman who tried to embarrass me in public for not being married at 27, had 3 daughters. All 3 of them were married before the age of 20. One got divorced within 6 months. The second got divorced within a year and a half. The third had 4 kids and, although not divorced, she was busy at home with the kids while her husband was gallivanting with other younger girls.

What do I call that? Karma? I was sad for her daughters, although not for her!

Things have changed a little bit now, but this culture still exists in a lot of countries.

* *

Being Single and Facing the Reality
By Sutha Shanmugarajah

We have a tendency to judge people based on their outward appearance. What we see and what we hear from others greatly impacts what we think. Is it fair to form an opinion at this point? As the saying goes, "Don't judge a book by its cover." Every book is different and unique in its own way. Some are colorful and appealing to look at, while others are plain and not so appealing, but are those unappealing ones worth reading? The content of a book can be far more appealing than its attractiveness. In the same way, until we have the opportunity to get to know someone, is it fair to form an opinion?

I come from a culture where women should be married by the age of 25, or at least by 30. If you are not married by then, people start forming opinions about you, and start looking down on your family. Those that genuinely care about you, don't make too much of a fuss, but then there are others that like to point out your flaws to offer some sort of explanation. Are these people aware that they are hurting me? Have they ever questioned how they would feel if the tables were turned around? I have become the center of attention for negative conversation, and my family members constantly get badgered with questions such as, "Why hasn't your daughter settled down?" "Are you looking for someone for her?" "Does she not want to get married?" Is there a problem?" It has been going on and on for years now. I don't look forward to family functions anymore. The same questions keep coming my way. I wish I could cry out, "Please leave me alone and stop hurting me!"

"You will never understand the damage you did until someone else does the same to you; that's why I'm here." – KARMA

A woman who is not married or does not have any children is regarded as having no value. It doesn't matter what she does—she could be involved in other activities that help the less fortunate or be advancing her education for a better career—it is all admirable but yet of no worth. These people don't realize that marriage and kids is not for everyone. They make me feel as though I have a terminal illness.

Then there are men who think that single women in their 40s are available for free sex. In their minds, how could a woman survive without being in a relationship? They think that, like food, sex is necessary for survival—such a disgusting mentality.

Everybody is born in this world for a different purpose. Some people die at an early age, of disease, an accident, or for other reasons. People should be given the opportunity to live their lives as they wish. Unfortunately, people have embedded a script in their mind of how life should pan out, and are too quick to jump to conclusions when things take a different turn.

So, why do we need to go around and discriminate against people when we don't know what they are going through? Everybody is going through some problem, and it is a part of growing up and learning, so we should not discriminate against people if certain things are missing in their lives. The reason I wanted to share my experience is to show that these kind of circumstances and discrimination can impact a person mentally and emotionally. I am a strong woman who is capable of standing up for myself, but there are lot of other women out there, who would not be able to handle this.

I want to say to you all: Don't let anyone discriminate against you for any reason; fight for your right to speak up, and don't ever let anyone destroy your inner peace. We have the right to make our own choices, and we should be happy with them; nobody has the right to judge or discriminate against others.

Sutha Shanmugarajah
Community Service Ambassador

Notes

Notes

Notes

_____

_____

_____

_____

_____

_____

_____

_____

_____

_____

_____

_____

_____

_____

_____

_____

_____

_____

_____

_____

_____

Notes

_____

_____

_____

_____

_____

_____

_____

_____

_____

_____

_____

_____

_____

_____

_____

_____

_____

_____

_____

_____

_____

CHAPTER FIVE

MIXED RACE FAMILIES

"My mixed-race background made me a broad person,
able to relate to different cultures.
But any woman of color, even a mixed color,
is seen as black in America. So that's how I regard myself."
Alicia Keys

When You Are Born of Mixed Race

This one is also a doozy!

You always see these beautiful children and adults with distinct features.

Some happen to have parents from two different backgrounds and/or race, and you can imagine how distinct their looks are.

Some have parents of Asian and Black descent.

Some have parents of Asian and Caucasian descent.

Some have parents of Black and Caucasian descent.

Kids born of the above lineage, are apparently called "colored!"

As it turned out, I came to learn and experience it myself!

Read my story on the next page…

Colored? What Does It Even Mean?

Hanover, Germany

An extremely beautiful, and one of my favorite cities in Germany.

Back in the mid and late 80s, I frequently visited Hanover because one of my closest friends and her family lived there. I spent most of my annual vacation there; it was a lot of fun, and I have great memories.

I enjoyed going out with my friend and her siblings, cousins, and friends. We all loved music and dancing, so we went to nice clubs in the evenings. I was always asked to dance by strangers, which I politely declined, as I don't like dancing with strangers! At least that is my personality.

There were a lot of Germans and other Europeans, as well as a lot of Africans.

One year during my visit, only a couple of days after my arrival, someone told me, "Oh, the word is already out that the *'snobbish colored girl is in town!'"*

I was so shocked and a little surprised. Then I asked what the meaning of "colored" was since that was the very first time, I had ever heard the term "colored." The reply of how people saw it, at the time, really upset me! Casually, the answer was, "Oh, it just means that the person is considered a "bastard"—a child of mixed race i.e.: not black, not white; thus colored."

The saddest thing was that it was the Africans/Black guys who called me "snobbish colored girl!"

I then questioned myself: "I am not white, which means I am black, so why am I not accepted as a black person 100%?"

I was so mad, I had difficulty sleeping that night.

****

My close friend and I were in London, England in the late 80s. My friend lived in Germany (she is of mixed race and about a shade darker than me) and was a map guru, while I was a "let's take a taxi" kind of girl, as I hated maps.

We had purchased tickets to attend Stevie Wonder's concert. He was performing in London at the time of our visit, and my friend insisted on not spend money on cabs, and that we should leave early and go by train.

At one point, she decided to ask about a certain street, and two older English ladies were walking toward us, so she got closer to ask them while holding the open map in her hands. Do you know what happened?

They both screamed and ran! Because we were black ladies!

****

In 2009, my son and I went to visit my close friend and her family in Erding—a beautiful little city by Munich's airport.

I had major stomach pain and asked my friend to take me to the pharmacy.

There was no parking, so I told her to stay in the car, and I got out and walked to the pharmacy. The pharmacist guy stared at me like I was a ghost of some sort. I said hello—no answer. I then slowly told him that I needed something to help with stomach ache. He still stared at me and gave no answer. I asked him if he spoke English—no answer. Then another gentleman walked in and was looking at the over-the-counter medications. He heard me say, "Are you telling me that you are a pharmacist and don't speak English?" And once again, I got no answer.

Then the man who had just walked in (who was also German) came to me and said that he could help. I told him what I needed, and he told the pharmacist in German. He then smiled and gave me the meds. I paid, thanked the man who had helped, and walked out.

I told my friend that I needed to go back to that place to tell off the pharmacist before I returned to Canada! She laughed and I never did.

****

In January 1997, I immigrated to Canada.

In my very first year in Toronto, one evening, I was watching comedy on TV.

The comedian said, "This black lady was photocopying these papers, and she ain't even black—she was colored...." And that was the second time that I had heard it. Little did I know that I would hear it many, many times later in my life.

I was at a job once, where a conversation started (I was the only black), and during our talk, I said, "As a black woman..."—they all then jumped on that, saying that I was not black!! When I told them, "Well, I am not white, so what does that make me?" They said they didn't know but insisted that I was not black.

That conversation was annoying (at least for me).

Keep reading...

****

I Never Thought About Giving My Adopted Daughter "The Talk"
By Mike Huggins

It took me years to realize it, but I finally understand that I am the poster child of white privilege. You see, on paper, I had it all: an MBA from the Wharton School, a fast-tracked path up the corporate ladder, prestige, and power. I had the wife, the house, and two beautiful kids. I also had the perks and ego that came along with being an executive.

I also thought that I was one of those "woke" white folks. You see, on many levels, I could check the boxes:

- My wife and I had adopted Adrienne, a mixed-race daughter, as an infant.
- We have a white, biological daughter, Katherine, and believed this would bring balance and perspective in dealing with racial disparities.
- We raised both of our girls to treat everyone as equals.
- We moved from New England, to a suburb of Philadelphia, so that she could grow up in a more diverse environment. (There was definitely more diversity than New England as it was clearly a white-dominated environment.)

We provided what we believed was a race-neutral environment, along with the perspective that everyone is to be respected and honored regardless of race.

But the warning signs that race and discrimination were indeed a factor affecting Adrienne's upbringing, started as an infant, and continued through high school and beyond.

At our local playground, Adrienne was usually the only person of color. Inevitably, someone would question why she was there and where her parents were. She would innocently point in our direction, but we could see the angst and frustration on their faces, that someone "different" had invaded their space. On more than one occasion, I had to defend myself and Adrienne. Nothing even remotely close to this ever happened when her sister, Katherine, went to the park.

A few years later, Adrienne was walking our dog in our upscale neighborhood, when she was accosted by a neighbor demanding to know why she was in the neighborhood and threatening to call the police. After explaining that she was walking the dog in her own neighborhood, the angry woman didn't believe her and demanded to know what dog service she worked for. Obviously, being distraught, Adrienne came running home, and I went running up to the neighbor to set her straight. Of course, once I explained that she was my daughter, she apologized. Too little too late, as the damage was already done to Adrienne, who was getting a firsthand education about inequality and racism.

Adrienne is a natural athlete, and she excelled in soccer and lacrosse. Due to her light complexion, most of the adults thought she was Columbian, and they went out of their way to invite her to their Columbian children's play groups. While this sounds innocent enough, Adrienne was a bit perplexed in asking, "If there are Columbian play groups, why aren't there play groups for mixed or black children?"

In elementary school, she asked a simple yet profound question: "Dad, why do my white friends live in big houses, and my black friends live in small apartments?" I gave her an answer but must admit that it wasn't very informed.

After receiving her driver's license, she complained about being pulled over by the police multiple times while driving with her black friends, but never with her white friends. Unfortunately, I kind of shrugged off this question and turned it around with, "What were you doing wrong?" It never occurred to me that perhaps she was being targeted and hassled because of her skin color.

Adrienne has grown into a wonderful woman, full of joy, passion, and integrity. Her coming of age coincided with the evolution of the Black Lives Matter movement. After being moved by and participating in the BLM protests, Adrienne had an epiphany about her identity, and she felt a call to action. This resulted in a series of uncomfortable conversations about race and privilege. These conversations should have occurred years ago; but unfortunately, I was blind to seeing things other than from a privileged perspective. Although I should have been the one who initiated this conversation, I am grateful that she spoke up to express her frustrations.

Her first question was simple yet deep: "Dad, why didn't you ever give me the 'driving while black' talk?" These few words went to the heart of the issue, as I had never considered the possibility that racism could live so close to home. I never considered that the police may not be looking out for you, but rather they might be looking for you! She talked about feeling pressure to represent her race, and how the media reinforces racial stereotypes. We talked openly about how racial discrimination affected her life on a daily basis.

Her tone was not emotional but rather matter of fact, about something she had clearly been living with her entire life.

Discrimination for one person may look like privilege but not for another. Along with privilege comes the responsibility to listen, learn, advocate, and become part of the solution. I have come to realize that even though both daughters were raised in the same household, by the same loving parents, they had profoundly different experiences. Knowing that there are other "Adriennes" in the world, gives hope that real change can happen. Change will occur if we continue to have these uncomfortable conversations, and use our privilege to be part of the solution.

Michael D. Huggins is the founder of *Transformation Yoga Project,* a non-profit organization serving people impacted by trauma, substance abuse, and incarceration, through trauma sensitive yoga programs. Mike received prison time for a white-collar misdemeanor, where he saw firsthand the discrimination of people of color. He is also the co-author of the book, *Yoga for Recovery: A Practical Guide for Healing.* He is the father of two daughters.

****

Why Do I Look Different?

I always asked myself this while growing up, although I never verbalized it out loud.

Growing up with a single mom (at least from the age of almost 6), I never knew anything better. Most importantly, I never knew why my features and my hair was different than most of my friends, my neighbours, and school mates.

Ethiopians and Eritreans mostly have a straight nose, beautiful features, and mostly wavy and curly hair. I, on the other hand, had a flat nose, and long, straight hair.

I remember a lot of the girls always asking me where my father was, and I had no answer since my mom completely refused to discuss this particular subject with me. So, I had no answer for the girls, which always made me feel sad. They also always wanted to play with my hair, as it was long, and that was annoying most of the time.

The first 12 years of my life, I went to a private, Italian-run Catholic School; but from grade 7 onwards, I was moved to public schools, as Mom could no longer afford to pay for both me and my brother.

My struggle started in public school where the boys were always making fun of my nose and even my hair! The bad kids told me that I was probably a "bastard" since I didn't have a father! It was painful!!!

I used to go home and stand in front of the mirror, staring at my features. I would ask myself, "How come I don't look like any of my friends?"

I didn't quite grasp the fact that I was actually born of a mixed race, until our return to Sudan (where I was born), after the civil war in Ethiopia/Eritrea, when I found out that my dad was not Ethiopian. He was of Turkish origin and had grown up in Sudan, and that was where my parents had met. I also learned that my great grandmother was Moroccan!

Many, many times, when in Sudan, I was called "Al habashiya" which translates to "Abyssinia," by *some* Sudanese females (even co-workers) who had something against Ethiopians/Eritreans, and because my mom was Ethiopian! For them, in their ignorance, calling an Ethiopian or Eritrean "Al habashiya" was an insult! The more I heard those whispers, the more I became proud of who I was and where I came from.

I don't think some people have any idea how painful and depressing it is when you get called names, are discriminated against, and are sometimes bullied!

****

My Life Experiences of Racism: A Recollected Synopsis
By Dr. Anthony Hutchinson

The year 2019 was my 52nd year of life. Who would have thought that 52 years after my 1967 birth year, I would still be encountering "in-my-face" racism in the most blatant of ways?

Even when on my most recent, July 2019, trip to Iceland, despite my first-class flight on Iceland Air, and my stay in a 4-star hotel, in Reykjavik, it was not enough to prevent me from being turned away from three empty local barbershops in a row, where all I was seeking was a beard shave. Their disconnected but consistently common reason was that they were all booked for the day, despite their shops being empty. The only person frequenting their shops, mind you, was me, a 6'2" person of color, seeking a beard shave—flanked by my petite, blond-haired, blue-eyed partner, who could only gasp at witnessing what racism was like for her beloved companion.

Needless to say, upon returning to Canada, I was blatantly racially-profiled by a Canada Border Services Agent (CBSA), and I called him on it as he had absolutely no reason to stop and question me, other than the fact that I was a big, tall person of color, accompanied by my petite, blonde-haired partner. Sadly, my latest episodes of "in-my-face racism" (four times over two days) was the icing on top of a lifetime mountain of experiences. Despite being a duly-qualified, highly-educated doctor of psycho-social clinical practice, as well as a multiple-time, court-qualified forensic assessor, my ongoing experiences of being a target of racism in my life are as constant today as they were from the times of my youth.

I can recall, in my Grade-1 year in elementary school, in Burnaby, B.C., when an older Caucasian boy, in the washroom, expressed to me: "If you wash yourself good enough, maybe you can get all that dirt off of your skin." Of course, the school itself did not help me out, as in my same Grade-1 year, a school social worker labeled me as being "mentally retarded." This caused me to be referred to the school board's clinical psychologist who diagnosed me, being the only brown boy in my Grade-1 class, as most certainly being mentally retarded. My mother refused to accept these misdiagnoses and took me to my family doctor, who reported that I could not see the blackboard in my class— not because I was a brown-skinned, mentally retarded boy, but because I needed glasses due to having severe myopia.

By Grade-4, despite being the best floor hockey goalie and soccer goalie in my school, my Grade-4 teacher opted to bench me, to the ardent protests of my classmates and much of my supporting school peers, in favor of a Caucasian classmate of mine, who completely demonstrated that he was a poorer goalie in both sports compared to me.

By Grade-7, Caucasian girls in school mocked me as the only, brown-skinned boy in my class, and splashed my white uniform shirt for my Catholic school, with red paint. Then, in Grade 8, while I had a crush on a pretty blond girl in my class, and when

I went to give her one of my school photos, one of my "friends" passed by behind me and, within earshot of the girl, expressed: "Your picture seems a 'little dark,' doesn't it?" In the same school year, my class peers teased and jeered at me, giving me the nickname, "Abdul," despite my actual name being "Tony Hutchinson."

Even in my Pentecostal Church (where my mother insisted on taking my sister and I, as a safe and loving place), I was placed in a situation, whereby an older church boy said to me: "Hey, Paki, do you know what the difference between you and a bucket of shit is? The bucket" he jeered, before I could respond.

When I moved to Ontario, at the age of 19, my boss, at a Shoppers Drug Mart store (where I got a job as a stock clerk), referred to me as "J.B." — short for "Jungle Bunny." He also referred to me as "the rat" as he did not know where I came from. As a result of his mocking of me, other drug store staff often chimed in on a daily basis, making me feel all the more humiliated for my year-and-a-half stint in the drug store.

When I finally got into my BSW at York University, despite the school's progressive anti-oppressive stance, the Caucasian statistics professor, at the time, was consistently hostile to me as the only male person of color in his class, while he had a tendency to ogle many of my pretty young classmates. Likewise, when I was completing my PhD in the School of Social Work at Wilfrid Laurier University, my then Caucasian Research Methods professor expressed to me (after he learned I had received a tenure-stream job at another university): "Now that you got yourself a professor job, I suppose you no longer have to play the race card."

While all of these experiences of racism were indeed horrible for me, perhaps one of the most humiliating episodes occurred in or about 2004, when I was out with a group of my mainly Caucasian friends in downtown Toronto. I remember how sad I felt after we stopped to buy some "street meat" at a sidewalk hot dog vendor, and a seemingly homeless guy yelled at me: "Hey nigger, f- you and your hot dog." Not one of my "friends" said a word in my defense.

My further experiences of being racially profiled, by members of the Toronto Police Service (TPS) for "driving while colored," and other instances of being needlessly detained by border service agents, have been numerous. Simply stated, this happens despite my professional and academic status. Even in the university where I am employed as a Department Head and Program Chair in Health & Human Services (and I hold the rank of Associate Professor), one of my dear colleagues came up to me at a student recruitment event and said: "Anthony, there is a young black girl over there; maybe you could go talk to her." He meant no harm.

Dr. Antony Hutchinson
BSc (Psychology), BSW, MSW, PhD
Doctor or Psycho-Social Clinical Practice
Forensic Assessor, Case Manager, Epidemiologist

Notes

Notes

_____

_____

_____

_____

_____

_____

_____

_____

_____

_____

_____

_____

_____

_____

_____

_____

_____

_____

_____

_____

_____

_____

Notes

Notes

CHAPTER SIX

STATUS, DISABILITY, AND APPEARANCE

"No matter our social status,
or how powerful we may be, we are all equal.
We came to this Earth empty, and we will leave empty.
When we die, we will get judged by our deeds only!"
Gaby Abdelgadir

Made Fun of for Not Having the Status

Here are a few stories from my interviews:

****

Being so young and innocent, I made a big mistake once by telling one kid, who I thought was my friend, that I was living in a foster home and hadn't seen my parents for a long time. I also told him that my dad was in prison for violence.

What happened the next day was a day that I will never, ever forget!

It turned out that the kid I shared my story with, told a few of the other kids, and everyone was looking at me funny in the class. At first, I wasn't sure what was going on, or why they were staring at me in a weird way, but I was about to find out soon enough!

At recess time, a few of the kids cornered me and said, "Hey, foster boy!!" and they all laughed at me. "Is that why you never change your cheap, dirty clothes, and you smell weird sometimes? Ha Ha Ha!! And why is your dad in prison? Did he kick your stinky butt?" And they said a lot more.

I remember that I ran out of school crying and didn't return until the next day! The kid I had trusted came to me apologizing, and told me that he spoke to the other kids and told them not to bother me anymore. But the damage was done!

Ever since that, I isolated myself, and there were times that I wanted to die. I started staying in class at recess, and would run out after school. It took me over a year, since that incident, to gradually start playing outside with other kids.

****

We were in Grade-7 when one day at recess, we were sitting eating snacks, and the conversation turned out to be about what our parents did for a living.

One of the kids who was raised by a single mother, said that his mom was an accountant and worked for a big accounting company.

Another kid said that his dad was a businessman and that his mom helped in the business.

The next one said that his dad was a lawyer and that his mom didn't work as she was taking care of the family.

When it was my turn, I said that my dad was a taxi driver. The kids went quiet, stared at me for a few seconds, looked at each other, and then started laughing! When I asked them what was funny, one of them answered: "That is not a job!" When I answered that of course it is, they all laughed again!!! Ever since that, they made fun of me and my dad, for quite a while. They treated my dad's work as if it was shameful!

I didn't say anything to my dad, but I did tell my mom. She was upset and told me that at least my dad works for himself and doesn't have to report to anyone. He can take vacation anytime he wants, without having to ask for anyone's permission.

My mom's response and explanation made me feel much better, and instead of feeling shame, she helped me feel proud!

****

My parents and two sisters lived in one of the so-called Metro-housing buildings until I went to college. During junior and high school years, my sisters and I were treated as low level (and underprivileged), as our parents didn't own a house or a car. It was not a nice experience. Some (not all) of the students' parents wouldn't even want us in their homes.

I remember once when a classmate asked me, "Don't all the

drug dealers live in those buildings?" I had never heard that term before until she said it.

My parents were hard workers and made sure that we got all we needed for our education, something I took very seriously, and I swore to myself that after I graduated and got a good paying job, I was going to move my family and buy my dad a car. And I did!

From all the experiences we went through, my sisters and I have learned never to judge people, and to always be kind and helpful to all humans, especially the underprivileged!

* *

Most of my friends in school wore designer clothes. Their running shoes were worth over $300! I always wore non-designer shoes, mostly from Walmart and the like. So, many times, I was a joke and was made fun of because of my "cheap" shoes and clothes.

As soon as I turned 15, I got a part-time job at a grocery store, saved my money, and bought my first expensive running shoes for a little over $200. I still became a joke for wearing my first "good" shoes.

What I learned over the years, no matter what you try, you can never win! So, I stopped shopping for expensive stuff, and saved my money for a car.

* *

Disability and How Some People Are Treated

Humans can be really harsh!

Growing up, I heard kids and adults being called names. "Hey, you, 'one leg!'" is one example, for someone who had lost a leg. People would be having a conversation about an event or about someone, and instead of calling them by their names, they referred to them by their disability! The blind one, the four-finger one, the mentally retarded one, the crazy one—the list goes on!

I also have heard stories of people who would abandon their child if he/she were born deformed in any way.

So many parents who had a disabled kid, used to hide their child at home to avoid the bullying in the outside world!

When I was around 15 years old, we had a neighbor who was pregnant, and I remember that her husband used to beat her from time to time, and we would hear her scream. One day, her husband was beating her and, to add to that, he said to her, "If you deliver a disabled or ugly child, I will divorce you!" Can you believe that?

I remember that my mom picked up something that was made of heavy metal, and she went to the husband and said to him, "If you ever touch her again or insult her in any way, I will smash your head with this!" I was horrified!!! The guy was shocked and stared at my mom, and then asked, "Roma, you would really do that to me?" My mom's reply was, "Try me!!"

We never heard any more screaming or insulting, at least not up until we moved countries. You never messed with my mom (RIP Mama).

I am so grateful to see that there is now a lot of help for disabled kids and their parents.

****

Here, I will share a few of my random conversations:

****

I was in the subway one day, on my way home from work, and an older lady was limping and carrying a heavy bag. I could tell she was struggling, and I offered to help carry her bag for her until the train arrived and she got a seat. At first, she looked at me strangely (maybe because I was black). I smiled and told her not to worry, and that I was a good person and was just trying to be helpful. After a bit of hesitation, she agreed and handed me her bag.

Once the train arrived, we got in, and there was only one seat, on which I made sure she sat. I stood not far from her, and she kept staring at me, and each time I smiled. After a few stations, the guy beside her left, so I sat down. She then thanked me and told me that people treated her so badly most of the time.

"You know, never mind helping me with whatever I am carrying; when I get on the bus or the train, even if they see I am limping, rarely does anyone offer me a seat. In fact, some give me a weird look! So, I really appreciate what you did." I then asked her how she had hurt her leg. "Oh, my right leg is shorter than the left one; that's why I walk like that. I was born that way." I asked her how she had dealt with it in school in her younger days, and her reply was, "OMG, don't even get me started! The bullying I had to go through! Some kids can be so harsh. A lot them called me names and made fun of me to the extent I didn't want to go to school, but my parents encouraged me. I could tell you stories for a whole day!" she giggled.

It was time for me to get off at my station, and I hugged her and told her that she was beautiful, and that she should never worry about how people look at her.

I am sure I made her day, but most importantly, I felt really good for bringing a smile to her face.

* *

Another huge problem that humanity is facing is "mental health."

- Depression
- Fear
- Anxiety
- Anger

The number of youngsters going through any of the above, is tremendously increasing.

The saddest thing is that families who have healthy children do NOT have any understanding of how serious mental health is.

Some even gossip about other people's kids: "He/she is useless and is not doing well in school. He/she is weird." They keep badmouthing and gossiping about families instead of trying to understand (that's if they care at all) the issues they are going through.

How many kids have committed suicide due to mental illness?

Why does it happen? Is it because no one is noticing their silent suffering? Is it because no one cares? Is it due to job loss? Or is it because they are being discriminated against or being bullied for one reason or another?

We all need to be more attentive and more sensitive when dealing with anyone that is struggling with mental illness, instead of gossiping about them or ignoring them totally!

All those suffering from depression, fear, or anxiety, need more love, support, and understanding!

Notes

_____

_____

_____

_____

_____

_____

_____

_____

_____

_____

_____

_____

_____

_____

_____

_____

_____

_____

_____

_____

Notes

Notes

Notes

_____

_____

_____

_____

_____

_____

_____

_____

_____

_____

_____

_____

_____

_____

_____

_____

_____

_____

_____

CHAPTER SEVEN

TIME TO BRING AWARENESS, EQUALITY, ACCEPTANCE, AND RESPECT

"One book, one pen, one child,
and one teacher can change the world."
Malala Yousafzai

Learn to ACCEPT, LOVE, and RESPECT Individuals for Who They Are

Our world is not going to evolve for the better until we all decide to change our perspective on how we see ourselves and others, and how we treat others. We must understand that we are all human beings and equal.

Every single issue brought to the surface to be resolved, requires awareness, perception, and a call to action in order to anchor the type of life we want to co-create.

We can begin this transition at home by showing and teaching our children to love and accept all people that seem different than them. Kindness dissolves aggression, judgement, competition, separation, assault, and any distractive actions. Let's bring light into every dark corner and co-create our new world.

Awareness through our different communities, like churches, mosques, synagogues, and all other cultural community centers, is fundamental in eradicating this disease called discrimination. As the saying goes, "Knowledge is Power." I believe this subject should be included in the school curriculum. Let us bring compassion, balance, equality, and justice into our education system, for our children are the future.

Every citizen can be active and participate in preventing and ending any bullying and abuse based on discrimination, whether it is because of skin color, race, religion, or status. It is our purpose in society to observe, prevent, and protect each other. Get involved in creating a safe, harmonious environment that we crave as humans.

A zero-tolerance policy for any kind of discrimination should be applied without any doubt, continuously and conscientiously. So many children and adults suffer, develop mental illness, and end their life because they are picked on and bullied.

Our system right now is not active or strong enough in helping the victims, or the perpetrators as well. Bringing awareness and education to every corner of the planet, on the negative side effects of any kind of discrimination, whether physical, mental, or emotional, is crucial. We have become accustomed to destruction and dysfunction in all our systems; let's wake up. It is every person's birthright to have equal rights, equal opportunities, equal treatment, and justice, freedom, acceptance, peace, and harmony.

IT MUST STOP AND BE TRANSFORMED TO KINDNESS!

Just imagine a world full of kindness, peace, acceptance, love, and respect for one another, living in balance and unity.

We can do it; united, we can thrive. A shift in our consciousness can lead us to freedom from all negative behaviors, habits, and actions that we inherited.

Let us remove all our blinders to help humanity see things clearly. It is time for co-creation and transformation for a United World! Let us remove the heaviness and illuminate the Planet. Let us plant the seeds of TRANSFORMATION!

****

Every small act that brings a positive change, makes the World a better place.

Every small step toward bringing equality to all, makes the world a kind place.

Every small thought toward helping another, makes the World a safe place.

Every kind word to another, makes the world a peaceful place.

Every person makes a difference in the World!

Every person counts and matters in the World!

****

Notes

Notes

_____

_____

_____

_____

_____

_____

_____

_____

_____

_____

_____

_____

_____

_____

_____

_____

_____

_____

_____

_____

Notes

ABOUT THE AUTHOR

Gaby Abdelgadir lives in Toronto, Ontario, Canada.

She has lived in 3 different countries prior to immigrating to Canada, and her experiences with discrimination, be it for herself or witnessing it happen to many others, led her to become passionate about fighting for equality, acceptance, and respect.

Gaby is an international bestselling author who is constantly and tirelessly making a difference in the world.

Gaby is an advocate for equality, fairness, and kindness in the world by bringing awareness to all, regarding our prejudices and their impacts on society.

By writing this book on discrimination, it shows her commitment, dedication, and passion to touch people in a positive way.

As you read this book and all the inspiring stories, you will understand the kinds of discrimination that cause separation, division, aggression, violence, abuse, war, rejection, arrogance, and hatred.

We are programmed by our nation, culture, parents, and environment to discriminate against certain things and people, often unconsciously, which results in our specific behavior toward others.

You might even relate to some of the stories in this book, or you might have an "aha" moment that we are all human, equal, and deserve the same rights and treatment.

Gaby is a motivational speaker and a certified Canfield Success Principles trainer, helping individuals get from where they are to where they want to be.

Gaby is also a certified "The Linn Method of Clutter Clearing," and along with her Feng Shui skills, she will help you declutter your home, mind, time, and relationships.

Website:	www.thebookondiscrimination.com
	www.totaldeclutter.com
FB:	https://www.facebook.com/GabyAMula/
Twitter:	https://twitter.com/GabyAMula
Instagram:	https://www.instagram.com/gabyabdelgadir/
LinkedIn:	https://www.linkedin.com/in/gaby-abdelgadir-int-l-best-selling-author-83855271/

Manufactured by Amazon.ca
Bolton, ON